Guest of Myself

Poems Of

John Grey

Contents

Guest Of Myself

I'm at this party,
so loud, so crowded,
my mind can't help but
be elsewhere/

Music batters ear-drums.
Conversation screams out to be heard.
Bodies bump against each other.
And alcohol is two parts drunk, one part worn.

Luckily,
I am silent, alone, sober
and talking to a toadstool.

A woman asks me,
"Are you enjoying yourself?"
I often wonder
who else is there to enjoy.

Stone

I am a stone,
the lowest form of creation.
I'm granite,
a combination of quartz,
feldspar and biotite minerals.
I can only be moved
by outside forces,
from some brat of a kid
tossing me at his sister
to seismic donnybrooks
down below.
Otherwise, I am strictly inert.
I could have fallen from the sky
or been part of the rubble
from a long-ago Ice Age.
What do I know?
I'm dense. I'm thick.
I've none of the five senses
and as for feelings -
where do you think the term
"heart of stone" comes from?
I am undeniably old
but that's brought me no wisdom.
No arms, no legs,
no muscle, no brain,
I can't do a damn thing but sit here.
You've heard the phrase,
"Written in stone."
I guarantee I didn't write it.

The Mistress's Lament

Late at night.
she wonders about him.
He's living in another city now
which may as well be another continent.
When she says its name.
it seems so far far away.

She hopes he's doing well at his new job.
She's still concerned about
those pains in his joints.
She even finds herself concerned for his kids.
But not his wife.
She can see the two of them at the table.
Mona's prepared his favorite dish.
His lips smack their way into a compelling smile.
Mona beams.
Dammit!
Why must even her imaginary casserole
taste so good.

To think.
this was a man who once made
any excuse to slip away,
who rejoiced in the freedom
of kissing someone
who actually kissed back.
Her fingers massaged those aching shoulders.
Her soft words brought calm to that throbbing head.

And now. the one who asked for nothing in return
has been gifted with exactly that,
plus too many extra pounds, a matronly appearance,
strands of gray perverting her nut-brown hair.

Maybe he thinks everything about them
was so implausible., it never really happened
Yet they were joined -
joined yet if only he could see.

And she knows things his wife will never know.
About herself mostly.

My Annoying Self

"What day is it?" I ask my wife.
I know the answer.
But the question is, does she?
"It's your birthday," she says.

I will not let her off easily.
"So how old am I?"
She does the math in her head
and arrives at the answer, "50."

I do not indicate if she is correct
but continue on with my interrogation.
"And what did you buy me for my
fiftieth birthday?"

An odd look precedes her response of
"I bought you absolutely nothing
because you are not fifty
and it is not even your birthday."

She finally confesses that she
doesn't know what day it is.
That's when I explain that it's the 75th
anniversary of the 18th amendment's repeal.

She often says that all this trivia
is enough to drive her to drink.
"At least you won't be breaking the law,"
    I add.

This Trunk Must Never Be Removed

A cobweb veils the attic window.
Wind blows through the cracks,
blows the threads around
but can't undo what the spider has weaved.
Beneath the skylight, an old trunk rusts.
Its contents are lumped together, year on top of year.
A stained wedding dress. Newspaper clippings.
Yellowed letters. Faded photographs.
What, I wonder, does the ephemera of former lives
hope to achieve.
I prefer the good work of the spider.
the ceaseless endeavors of the deathless.
But I've been informed that these are family heirlooms.
The ancient diary is a treasure, even more so
with the petal fossil pressed between its pages.
They tell me that it doesn't matter that its ink is melting
So I don't mention that the binding needs regluing.
But I suppose when we go wordless, heartless,
we can't help but stroke the guilt of those who come after.
And we leave behind a ball of string in the assurance
that it will encourage the living to love the dead.
Stuff like this is the past's currency,
like the bronze shoe that stands in
for the cute little toes of a long line of babies.
But, as cash in hand goes, it doesn't buy me anything.
But look at the web. It's flouncing like a lacy petticoat.
Bugs bob at the edges. The arachnid will eat them in time.
No insect remains for the endless enjoyment of offspring.
Just a no man's land. And there's no better definition

for this ugly tin-type, this post card from the Atlantic City void.
The spider gives me a hard look. This is his territory, not mine.
He lives in the present. In the creep of light across dusty air.
In whatever it takes to survive and breed.
And objects take up space which is all they know to do.
And silver-tongued mothers tell me this human fungus matters.
Truth is, we can't stay behind no matter how much stuff
we shove into boxes and drawers.
Time must involve itself strictly in those still living.
Really, it can only do so much.

Poetry Class

He loved to teach, so he said.
He knew much about poetry.
And poets too.
And not just the usual stuff
but the scandal.
Who slept with who and why not.

My favorite was the torrid affair
between Verlaine and Rimbaud,
all that absinthe and hashish,
madness and violence, sex and scandal.
And yes, I do believe that both were guilty
of writing the odd verse.

And he implored us to write our own.
He'd give us a word to get started.
Then he'd play music -
Debussy was a favorite
but also weird jazz
like Ornette Coleman.
The idea was to inspire us
or, as he put it,
disinfect we pour souls,
kill off all the cautionary bugs,
the old-school lice.

Most of the stuff our class churned out
was crap of course.
He'd examine each piece of work in turn,

scream out things like
"third rate Bukowski"
or "rhyme slime,"
screw up the paper
and toss it at the wall.

To be honest
I learned nothing about poetry
from his class.
But if it wasn't for him,
I never would have written this.
Same as if it was for him.

Maine

It'd be a land of giants
except they sink into the mud.
Or wherever they stand,
the spruce stand taller.
And when they speak,
it's like their jaws
have been shot up with Valium.
"Muthah, Fathah,
where's the cah?"
Chowdah, ayuh,
gawmy, crittah...
you get the idear.
Nobody there
has ever lived anywhere else.
"Californier - all that
yoger shit and movie stahs."
There's fishing villages
the color of the fish they catch.
And houses stacked on
wave-wracked rocks.
Somewhere in the middle
is Stephen King
and beyond him,
bears and moose.
The sun gets there first
for some reason.
But it don't stay long.
The only one syllable state -
has to be if you want

to be a Mainah.
I met a woman from there once -
away from the trees
and with the mud off her shoes
and quiet when I held and kissed her…
well maybe she wasn't from Maine
after all.

Watching The Monarchs

On a meadow at wood's edge,
June floats in on black and orange wings,
completes Spring's promise,
fuels Summer's largesse.

My eyes have their wish -
the monarchs have arrived.
Such a will to live.
Scraps of creature
cheating the wrecking ball of weather
from far down south
all the way to my doorstep.

What is sadness compared to this?
Deft as a ballerina's toes
or a deaf man's fingers,
they find, in air, a secret language,
writ from buttonbush to aster.

Beyond prevailing platitudes,
delicate purpose becomes beauty.
Instinct rivals even love.

Get Born Why Don't You

The child is late.
Your entire body is getting on your case -
night agony, morning nausea.
Birds flock to the feeder,
sing the hallelujahs
of eggs so easily laid.
Birth, for them, is suddenly here,
then quickly gone.
You'd willingly sit in a nest if it were that simple.

Sun sweeps the bedroom floor.
You conduct so much energy
that you don't care anymore
that you're a swollen blimp
piloted by one determined to stay put.

Two kids from prior years
want you to understand their needs.
Noise is the prominent tool in their trade.
Your husband struggles to make their breakfast.
He's a protective force cracking at every seam.
Wait a minute, you remind yourself.
There's a beauty here,
a phoenix will rise from floppy, bloody ashes.
Soon enough, pleasure will oust pain.
The world's not so cruel
as to condemn you for doing its bidding.

I Saw Ray

I saw Ray today in passing,
cigarette dangling from his lips,
Adonis handsome, a remarkable figure of a man.
Why I'm telling you this
is beyond me.

For your place is here,
not with Ray
but sharing time and space
with your romantic night-owl
to whom you turn
when the day's exhausted,
as it always is this time of night,
as we conclude, with a vengeance,
this meandering, meaningless day,
me reading the poetry of Shelley,
you in your down-dog yoga pose.

Peace comes in droves:
line after line,
stretch after stretch.
And who cares that our guy lost
in the governor's race.
And your mother's not well
and can't come to the phone.
Or that Ray is the guy you dated
before we met.
The evening is in a good place,

between the last of the dishes wiped clean
and the baseball scores from the west coast.

I wrap myself in "The Hymn To Intellectual Beauty"
and almost shriek and clasp my hands in ecstasy.
You're in a state where you either
go head-to-head with nirvana
or yap like a terrier.

This is a grace period for love.
Aside from Ray,
we have nothing else to go by.

Mood For You

It's either that
or the narrow shoreline,
and the ocean waves,
all that lapping 'and buffeting,
the raw smell of salt.

If it wasn't for that
other kind of appetite,
I'd be all about nature,
submerged one moment,
breathing warm air the next.

I can only make footprints
in the sand for so long
before something within yearns
to duplicate those steps
in your bedroom carpet.
And sun on my naked skin
is one thing.
But your fingers are ten things.

So I'm working up a need
other than avoiding jellyfish.
I'm seeking a-perspective
that doesn't have to end with the horizon.
Besides, it's getting late.
It's already dusk.
There's a seismic shift within me.

Don't be surprised if
I'm at your door step.
The tide has turned...
from the drug of the moon
to something more precious.

A Subway Muso

He plays saxophone
in the subway,
back to the wall,
face to the crowd.

His instrument
blows over and through
a wall of noise.
His face is contorted
by commuter shadows.

There have never been
so many people
whose hearing only extends
to their own thoughts
or the person standing next to them.

Even if the platform shook.
from a loud blast of brass,
they'd put it down to earthquake,
not music.

But sometimes,
the underground jolts just enough
for a coin or two
to fall from a hand,
drop into his cup.

His time,
though ignored or unnoticed,
is not wasted.

The Rhino

The zoo's sole rhinoceros
is nibbling hay, munching carrots.
Its company is its own shadow,
crowding around its feet, its armored belly.

It has room enough to move about,
two baths, one mud, one water,
and an ample supply of food
and 24/7 medical care.

My Aunt Rosie would be jealous.
She'd willingly give up freedom
to be so lovingly taken care of.
Like the time she lay in hospital,

nurses, doctors, at her beck and call,
meals served promptly three times a day,
TV perched on the wall above,
adjustable bed, phone at her side.

The family were concerned
that she was dying.
They didn't understand.
She was really living.

But Aunt Rosies aren't under
threat of extinction.
The rhino's unaware of his breed's fate.
So I interpolate the concern

into his dour expression.
And no one really knows
if he prefers it here
to his birth home on the African veldt.

So, once again,
I do his thinking for him.
Look at those sad and weary eyes.
They need a refresher course in freedom.

And the slow, stumbling gait.
He longs for vast plains to open to him.
And his long, sorry stare in my direction,
the realization that I'm no potential mate.

But his native land is rife with poachers.
Any one at any time could take him out.
And the zoo is a hive of anthropomorphism.
The rhino in my mind can't tell the difference.

Meet The Folk

The foam coffee cup in the holder
looks down at three squashed ones
on the floor of his truck.
Dorito crumbs line the seat cushion.
He holds the local record
for most beef jerky swallowed in an hour,
is a regular at Wednesday's two-for-one burrito night,
can drink just about anybody under the table
and swear like Woody Harrelson on a bad day.

Big hands ripple up to a tattoo of a devil on one arm,
a faded tribute on the other to some woman
who, you confess, is not your mother.
The parlor of your house is littered
with back issues of Hot Car Magazine and Garth Brooks cd's.
And he owns a jacket that's actually
studded with rhinestones.

And he's your old man.
This is what you have to accept
when it's time to bring a boyfriend home.
You dread what they'll think
of the fuzzy dice that hang
from the rear-view mirror of his truck.
Or the bumper sticker that reads,
"Gas or Ass No One Rides For Free."

How do you explain that,
somewhere in your DNA,

is an addiction to shotguns and monster truck shows?
And what if, in your father's cellar bar,
he spies the poster on the back wall,
and asks, "Who is Farah Fawcett?"

You're sensitive, articulate, curious,
well-read and ambitious.
Your dad's rude, belligerent,
and his favorite TV show is "Duck Dynasty."
You love each other despite each other.
And you never know,
maybe your new guy will like hand-fishin'.
Thanks to your dad,
you'll find these things out
before it's too late.
The Cicadas

Every thirteen years they emerge -
about as I often as Bert and me have sex
says Jessie.

According to the hook,
when it's time to mate,
males bang their cymbals.
and females flap their wings.

Well at least that means we're doing it right,
she adds.

Poem For It

There are those who say
it's a well-paying job
in the city.

Others that it's sex with a stranger
on a Saturday night.

Or a reconciliation
with a sister you haven't seen in years.

Whatever it is,
it has to be local,
at odds with what's going
on in the world.

A pearl crescent on a fluttering aster.

It could even be that.

Bobcat

It has no idea that,
as it trots across
the snowbound landscape,
there are other cats
curled up on a human's lap,
before a roaring fireplace.

For all it knows,
every feline must forage for food
in this desolate wilderness.
They have to be lean,
not fat.
Paying attention
not tribute.
For, even at rest,
a cat is still a hunter.

Day after winter's day,
the bobcat rummages
for vole and mole or mouse.

It's never seen a tiger
But it knows the feeling.
It's never seen a house cat.
Or imagined one either.

Gaits

My father could still walk
but barely, the day of the storm,
when we trudged home from the local bar,
and when huge drifts slowed me to his speed.

"Made for winter," he said, indicating
the grumbling bones in his legs.

Outside seemed impassable to me,
all forward journey sent back
by huge mounds
and cold, heavy blows of wind.

But he hummed an old song,
as if his bearing were there
between his tongue and his teeth.
He planted confident boot-prints
like he once put down seed.

As we stumbled home,
he kept up with me,
old rules of age, of balance,
broken with every step.

That was a month before he died,
when he came to life a little,
boasted proudly how he could still do it.

I stopped at the door
to wipe my boots on the mat.
He kept on going,
straight into the darkness.

Parental Visit

Nurses keep waking Matt
out of his coma
to tell him things that make no sense
to his lifeless brain.

They shake
his shoulders,
scream in his ear –
        your mother is here, Matt,
            your father is here, Matt.
How do you explain to someone
that you don't know what "here" means?

Matt has bulbous eyes
that are content to stare at the ceiling.
It has wonderful white cracks of paint.
And a battalion of spiders
that he marshals like a general.

But nurses insist on sitting him up,
twisting his head in all directions,
like they're lining up rifle sights.
Two strangers step through the door,
wide grins on their faces.
If he really was a gun,
he'd shoot them.

I Have A History

I have a history
but that should not impede the flow of conversation -
            however
            it does.
You chose to be with me
        no doubt suspecting you're not the first
while your virginity is as copious as the intelligence in your eyes.

I have a history
but a history is not always specific to your understanding of the
word –
            imagine a world
            without you in it.
    What would you expect me to do
    in such a situation?
As a doctor could tell you, though the symptoms may be similar,
        not every diagnosis is the same.

I have a history
but that's because I have always been this "I" thing,
            placed in situations
            where I am the only one.
There's no rule that encompasses everything from socio-sexual
mores to
            hormones to
            opportunity
to whatever people want of each other in the instant
        that is innately impractical in the long term.

I have a history
but more of affinities that allegiances, temporary accommodation,
            not permanent housing
            with wall-paper to match.
Life is this story with ten thousand plotlines –
       some feel inspiring in the writing
       but sordid in the telling.
I can keep them to myself but they'd still come out in your
assumptions.

I have a history
but more of a portrait of a younger self too easy with his affec-
tions,
            too eager to experience
            but not conclude.
For better or worse, it's what has got me here,
       to this moment, this place,
       with you,
and your nervousness and your love, your anxiety and your love.
I have a history
but, to be honest, it's not much of one, not as cavalier as you
imagine,
            more small doses of awkward passion,
            unrewarding romance.
I put down its flawed, unflattering timeline to not having met you
yet.
       And here you are with me,
       wondering is this where you want to be.
Yes, I have a history. But I also have a future. So shall we begin?

The Car Came For The Rich Kid

At high school, a car always came for the rich kid.
And girls flocked around him
though he really wasn't that good looking.
But he always dressed better than the rest of us.
And he had a wallet.
Whenever a dollar or two came my way,
I stuffed it down my pocket.

One day, the rich kid offered me a ride.
But I was too embarrassed
to tell his driver where I lived.
I just said, "My mother's coming for me"
though our family didn't own a car
and then, when that Caddy was out of sight,
I began my long walk home.

Every step I took made me that much poorer.
By the time I reached home, my legs were tired
and I owed just about everybody.

Picasso Dies At Fifteen

In an attic trunk, that coffin for everything but corpses,
I uncovered some of my first attempts at art:
class assignments, the same head drawn badly
on five separate occasions, and a couple
of blotchy water-colors, the death knell
of my aspirations to be the next John Constable,
some pastels that wouldn't have earned me a cent
doing quick sketches for beach tourists,
a botched shot at trompe l'oeil that looks more like
Donald Trump than any optical illusion,
and the usual unfinished stuff, doomed to remain incomplete
until the day that someone without my memories
tosses them into the trash.

I'm here to reclaim what is mine before the house is sold.
And certainly, my adolescence belongs to me.
That was my particular branch of self-discovery,
where I headed off in many directions at once,
one journey fashioning me with brush and easel,
a canvas, and two hands that failed to convince
my eye and imagination that they were up to it.
To be honest, these are not much better than the stick figures
I drew when I was seven, the entire family like
six toothpicks standing before a lopsided house
in the shade of a broccoli-shaped tree.
Ah youth, a time when we are best at what we're no good at.
For we have the ambition. We have the nerve.
And a battered old trunk for a time when we'll have neither.

And More Books

Sure these are books.
Books and books and more books.
Why have shelves
if you're not going to stock them
tighter than a rush hour subway train.
But they're also memories.
They're names and dates,
events even.
"Sorrows Of Young Werther"
has been with me
longer than any living soul.
"The Art Of Van Gogh"
is the baby in the family.
There are many I have yet to read,
some I will never read.
Many are like neighbors.
I nod a good morning
to "Finnegan's Wake."
I smile at "The Mysteries Of Egypt."
Some of these tomes
really are family.
My Thesaurus is like a smarter older brother.
My sisters are Dorothea, Rosamond
and Mary Garth from "Middlemarch".
And I'm the son of the Brothers Grimm
and Cinderella.
Some I've tossed along the way
but most stay with me,
give of their feelings

when mine are numb,
light up some dark corners
or show me how much blacker
it is elsewhere.
My wife wonders why
I don't thin them out,
keep only the favorites.
In other words,
what's with all this clutter?
She may as well ask,
what's with me.
A rhetorical question.
My books are with me always.

Identity

Come morning,
for a brief moment,
you're unknown to me.

In dream places,
I've been with dream people.
You were not among them.

My mind is temporarily unavailable.
A stranger occupies the tousled sheets.

Never touched this woman.
Nor threaded the hair with fingers.
Nor pressed my lips against her cheek.

My desire's waylaid by a phantom on a horse.
My pulse still beats for
the lady flaunting blue crinoline at the ball.

But then, summoned by the situation,
a name forms on my tongue.
I'm more and more confident enough to speak it.

"Hi," you whisper through your own personal fog.
You're at the end of your identification process.
I emerge clearly from the last time you saw me.

Side by side all night but only now are we together again.
You slowly rise. I follow. Another day
when a name is as good as any place to start.

Available For Cat-Feeding

Is there such a man
who feeds a woman's cats
while she's away in Florida for a week?
Yes, there is.
It's me.
I'm someone entrusted with the key
to another apartment
by a woman who worries not
that I'll steal something,
ransack her drawers, her closets,
or peek here and there
in search of secrets.
Tell me where the cat meat's kept
and I'm your guy.
Provide me with an inventory
of whose dish is whose
and I will fill them every day.
She warns me not to try
to get friendly with the beasts.
They've claws sharp enough
to crack walnuts.
In other words,
those animals will feast
on what I put out for them
but they won't show
the least sign of gratitude.
No purr to go along
with my fur-threading fingers/
No slalom rub

in and out of ankles.
Is there such a man
who will go all out for a woman
while knowing here will be no
commensurate reward?
I have filled that role forever it seems.
Relationships begin with
"You just don't know how much
I really need you."
They end with "Meow."

Crows

Crows are the most ominous
of birds.
They are not a choir
to which I ever can accustom.
Their caws don't meld
but face off against each other,
like pugilists of noise.
Add in their dark monk robes
and it all comes off as dirge.
The cemetery's the place for crows
but they perch on boughs
outside my window,
greet my morning
as if it's done already.

Marie

She was a nature lover
who never thought me green-blooded enough,
who figured my pale skin
should be more the color of dirt.
I remembered she was April
but the names of trees eluded me.
I picked a wildflower for her.
She informed me that I'd killed it.

She loved to ramble through the
woods for hours.
She despised the city.
Too loud, too busy, too smelly,
she said.
These were all my argumenta in favor.

She was as beautiful though
as the downtown at night after a rain shower,
soft and neon-colored,
sparkling where you'd least expect.
This comparison stayed with me.
Silent praise knows when it's well off.

Once she took in an injured owl,
nursed it back to flying.
This is why I never understood it
when she tried to clip my wings.

The Homes Of CEO's

They're always walled of course,
high enough so that only
the tip of the second floor
and the mansard roof is visible.
In medieval times,
a moat and drawbridge
would have separated them
from the commoners.
But they'd have been royalty then,
not MBA's.

It's a solid wall.
It's a wall that could have repelled armies,
kept those inside out of harm's way,
in another age.
I won't go into all of that
'built on the backs of workers' malarkey.
Such talk went out with Marx and Engels.

I prefer the simpler image
of a poet standing outside the large metal gates,
trying to get a better view that way
but the house blocked by trees.
Normally he would write about greenery
such as this.
But, in this case, he doesn't.

So nothing is risen from a mere seed,
stands tall in its trunk,

sighs in the wind, sheds resinous,
spreads branches wide and lush.

A poem about the home of a CEO
is ultimately a work
in which beauty is made meaningless
by connotation.
Only the wall emerges with any credit.

Obligations

I still return for the wakes, naturally.
Death can't keep me away.
I went back last summer
for the funeral of an uncle,
a brother of my late father,
the last of that line actually.
The last who saw action in a war.
The last who wore a hat and a tie clip on the job.
He was almost ninety, never married.
He quit school after grade 10
and went to work in the customs office.
I figured all those dirty books I longed to read
were stopped from entering the country by him personally.
My mother said, he was just a pencil pusher.
I still prefer my theory.
And yes, I put in an appearance at the weddings, also.
Bride's a second cousin, groom's my nephew -
if family needs me, I'm already on way.
A flight or a long car ride, one night in my old bedroom,
and then the journey in reverse -
my obligations come with their own Triptik.
My sincerest congratulations and my deepest sympathies -
that's all I need to pack.

Why I Won't Be With You At Christmas

On the one side there is my love
and on the other, your living arrangements.
My romantic soul is fully intact
and willing to take on all-comers
but if a heart can be susceptible to allergens
then your family is more than enough
cat hair, pollen and ragweed
to give it the most virulent of hives.
Your mother criticizes my supposed lack of ambition.
Your father looks down on me
like I'm something to be squashed, not embraced.
I'm sure your brother hates me.
And, though your younger sister sympathizes,
she keeps going on at me
about my lack of any tattoos.
Even your grandmother, when she's in residence,
is like this crackly-voiced PA system
continually announcing how short men's hair was
back in her day.
So while I appreciate you inviting me over
for this year's Christmas activities,
all I can say is –
    the roads are bad,
    more snow is forecast,
    I don't want to leave my sick mother all alone
    at this time of year,
    a cousin just died,
    I've contracted food poisoning
    etc etc etc

just remember, these are not excuses
born of lack of affection,
they're regrets based on past experience
and the knowledge that, though you love
your family dearly, that love is not transferable.
Remember, not all holidays are a time
to step away from the rigors, the ordeals,
the vicissitudes of life.
Some are a continuation.

Jenna Moves South

Palm trees are not new to her,
but now she lives with one,
a long leaning trunk,
a crown of leaves,
indifferent to the calendar.

Unlike the elms, the oaks,
she cannot gauge her mood by them.
No rush to bud,
no blossoming,
no contentment
at the fade, the fall, of beauty,
no resolve of bare winter boughs.

Strange how what doesn't waver
reminds her of all she has lost,
like the warmth that never knew
a cold day in its life,
the serenity unaware
of how it's earned.

But she won't be packing up,
going home any time soon.
She's made her decision.
Her life was once seasonal.
Now it's actual.
No coming, no going,
just here.

Arkansas Truck Stop

Must be morning
because the eggs
are sunny-side up,
the bacon's greasy,
and the hash browns
are near black.

Can't be home
because there's a huge trucker
on the stool beside me,
and two more in a booth.
Can't be home
because there's no way
I'd be kissing that cook.

Guy's got a pack of cigarettes
squeezed between his tee-shirt
and tattoo.
I read the local newspaper.
He skims the legs of the waitress.
One behemoth in the booth
can use the word 'rig' in a sentence.
Always prefaced by 'big' of course.

I'm out in the world,
Rayburns on the counter,
coffee passing on messages
to my senses.
It's just the one place.

It's just the one kind of people.
It's off a highway
some place in Arkansas.

And it must be real
because I know
I couldn't just write this.

The Shakespearean Actor

He's on stage, every night, playing grief,
be it Hamlet's for his father, Macbeth
at his vainglory or Othello's
hard look at his own reasonless rage.

But he puts so much into Shakespearean
misery that his personal anguish is
treated almost casually backstage,
a sip from a bottle as the makeup goes on,

two as it comes off. A fractured marriage
can't compete with the treacherous minxes
of the printed page. And what's a friend's
broken promise to duplicitous whispers

in the ear, a murderous stepfather.
His family aggravate him but their
ghosts don't appear on parapets.
And the news is never encouraging.

But it sure beats the cackling bile of witches.
He even considered suicide once.
Trouble was, he could never come up
with a soliloquy to rival, "To be or not to be."

One day, when he's much older, and his wife
has left him, and children seldom call, he'll be ready
to play Lear. Seven nights a week, a breakdown for the ages.
He'll have no strength left for his own tragedy.

.Artist And Model

He's been up all night.
Eyes still open.
Black coffee and pills at his side.

He's ensconced in his attic,
painting a body,
not just the grim features
but the stench as well.

The image takes shape.
More coffee. More pills.
Death is the subject.
The model's name is immaterial.

Splash and swirl,
spray and spackle -
he gets at the carcass
long before the worms and maggots.

The bloodiest red.
The darkest purple.
Blank eyes.
Pale cheeks.
Blue lips.
More coffee. More pills.

His smock is stained.
His teeth are yellow.
Hair flung back,

arms in constant motion,
his brow snaps with veins.

And the easel rocks unsteadily.
His palette colors ooze together.
His brush bristles are rougher
than the dark of his chin.

He's gulping coffee, popping pills,
rearranging the corpse...
it's the worst he's ever been…
it's the best thing he's ever done.

Jack Of All Trades

He can make bookshelves in his cellar,
shoot wild boar, raise old cars from
their deathbeds, climb mountains,
fashion a garden from just seeds and an idea.

Folks call him clever with his hands
though he reckons his mind's in there
somewhere also, hard at work, even if it doesn't
have time for gleaning facts from books.

I can call on him to fix a leaking tap,
replace a loose brick, extract a dead bird
from the chimney, even trap the squirrel
that's causing havoc in the cellar.

His is a world of tasks that need doing,
problems to be addressed, stuff that happens
to other people that only he can put right.
He's a need as much as he is a person.

He cleaned out my gutters for two beers
and the use of my bathroom.
No wonder I always feel like I'm getting
the better of the deal by far.

Same with the other folks who rely on him.
They're in debt to the guy to the point
where they resent as much as appreciate his help.
We can't pay him enough so he takes from our self-esteem.

It gets to the point where the roof leaks
and I don't even give him a call.
All day and night, droplets of water thump into a bucket.
I sleep soundly even if that sound keeps me awake.

Watching The Snake Charmer

A red-turbaned man
seated on a mat
in a rough-paved plaza
sways from side to side.
as he blows into his pungi.

From the raffia basket
at his feet,
a snake emerges,
an Indian Cobra,
uncoiling
a foot and a half
of vertical backbone.

Spectators watch in awe,
figure the sweet melody
is charming
even this most venomous
of killers
when it's the movement
of the instrument itself
that has the reptile
in its thrall.

The creature is
as deaf as my Aunt Gladys.
It figures the pungi
for a threat,
so it cocks

and spreads its head
in attack mode,
flutters its tongue,
hisses through
readied fangs.

So no,
despite what you've heard,
music does not soothe
the savage beast.
It merely suggests
the savage beast needs soothing.

The Kid

I walk slowly by the house
where I grew up.
A woman looks out the window
at me, suspiciously.
She must think I'm casing the joint.

In fact, I am.
I'm sneaking a peak
in through those
east-side facing louvers,
to see if I can catch a glimpse
of that kid bent over
a clunky Remington typewriter,
tapping away on the keys,
writing down the first thing
that breaks out of his gut,
jabs him in the heart,
or wrestles with his brain.

I'd like nothing more
than to break in,
say something like,
"Look at me kid.
This is where all of this will get you."

"So why don't you
go out and play with the other kids?"

If he thinks about it,
he's some other kid.
If he goes on typing,
he's me.

Michael's Music Lessons

Abused by keyboard,
cuffed round the head by keys,
his father had paid for the damn thing –
at least he was sending a monthly check
to the appliance store –
so somebody better be on that stool
and practicing their scales for hours.

He grew up terrified of music.
It was the monster that dwelled
beneath the shiny black lid.
Its claws were ivory.
Its mouth a heavy fallboard.
And, down below,
where his feet hung loosely,
pedals nipped at his toes.

But he survived.
Even played a mean "Fur Elise"
in his teens.
But his friends all craved guitars.
Saw them in store windows.
Not in nightmares.

The Time Of Your Child

Time is supposed to heal.
Maybe it just hasn't read up
on its job description lately.
The dead are as dead as they have ever been.
The surgeon's words still turn
his understanding into your bitterness.
A pale human face said sorry
when it should have been God.

Now every room is a wailing room,
even the silent ones.
Every other child
takes care to remind you of
but not be your own.
And the love of all these mothers
exhausts you.
They've no idea that the opposite
of three-year-old
is emptiness.

Then there's the time
that's your personal time,
the one that announces to you,
and you alone,
that it's time to move on.
This is time as starting gun
for some marathon
that you feel as if
you've already run.

And then there's your husband,
more caring than he's been in years.
He wraps an arm around you
every chance he gets.
This is time trying to make up
for all that it's lost.
The attention leaves you as cold as the fish in the freezer.
Can time do anything right, you wonder.

Hard Times

Got to keep taking anti-histamines.
I'm allergic to bats
and the mites that get in between
the quilt patches.
And I'm a something-or-other-philiac.
Apparently my kidneys
are as useless as emu feathers.
It could be from that tattooist
when he tried to initial my gut.
Besides, I can't get the smell of fish
out from my armpits.
Doctor wants to do tests
but I'll need to be scalped first.
That's sure to limit the number of times
I look in the mirror.
Doctors –
they're just madmen posing as mystics.
And always with the big tease.
"Maybe this will work."
So I'm spreading cream
across my stomach
and down my recommissioned legs.
And I'm lying in bed
with the curtains closed,
filtering daylight out of my world.
And beginning to realize
that all my passion
was merely transitory.
And sexual reflex actions

don't cut it any more.
I'm self-quarantined.
I'm like a bulb screwed into
the sockets of the sheets,
where the living and dead meet
and can never decide
who is who.
I got memories
like snails leave trails.
And quotations
that dissolve into cuss words.
Who wants company
when you impart
such cold and oiling films,
and the hymns you hum
are all to do
with barracudas and buggery.
So what's to eat?
More breadcrumbs?
How about a wash?
Now where did I put that sponge?
I survey my surrounds.
Unless a spider crawls across the ceiling.
there is never the slightest variation.
I prefer the dark.
That's where spurious notions go to die.
And I hate the future.
More dreams gone to hell.
More hope vandalized.
What can I say?
Me and the days to come have quite
a history.

Waking In A Fishing Village

"Don't bother to look," I warn you.
You're a stretch of my arm away,
cresting the warmth of my blood.
The name of this place is meaningless.
And there'd be no morning hug
but for bodies with people in them.
My half-vision lights you lighter -
don't worry, I've no vested interest in reality.
Outside, an old and bitter sea wind roars.
But in here, dreams have turned away from nothingness.
They've fastened doors and windows.
Now they open up,
breathlessly include you.
I catch your arm.
I don't speak, feel no need to eat.
I breathe heavily because
I've been all night in breathless nowhere.
Suddenly, my lungs know letter.
I'm in bed in our cottage.
Jackets in the closet,
zippers stare at me like cats' eyes.
Cheap framed prints look over me -
likewise, underwear in the drawer -
telephone, light switch,
ultimately streets and houses,
docks and boats -
a fishing village.
On a morning like this,
crooked cobblestone

clatters one life at a time,
any and all who've survived the night.
So who are we upon waking?
I pity the ones without you beside them.
You shine through the murk,
face swinging its lantern,
lips whistling old shanties,
The Dutchman is running.
The outside world's untenable.
There's a thick fog on the move
but a thin one where I lie.

Yours, Hilda

Please send me no more poetry.
Your stuff has deteriorated
so much of late that I cannot
bring myself to read it.
Where are the odes to butterflies,
the paeans for lost love?
Yes, 1loved the sonnets.
And I could deal with the free verse.
However this language junk
appalls me, likewise
the misappropriated beat.
Let's face it, you're
not Creeley, not Ginsberg.
You're not even you.
Yes, I could find other
uses for your recent stuff
but the texture is too rough
and I do not boast a fireplace.
I'm sorry our relationship
has to end this way
but what options do I have.
I remain but you do not apparently.

The Snail

sliming up
the dying rose
its wilted leaf

head emerges
from spiral-shaped whorls
of a snail's silvery shell

as it nibbles
unbothered
unhurried

like eternity
with an appetite

Gas Station

Straw hat's busted
and the blue and red flag's dragging on its pole.
The road's as narrow as a plumb line
and the sides are baked brick hard.
Rusty gas pump only offers regular.
In the window, brown and speckled eggs,
soda bottles, a can of oil.
Unshaven Ed flops in his chair out front.
Straw hat can't keep back July,
cakes his brow a stinky yellow.
A car creeps by but doesn't stop.
Maybe can't read the price of gas.
Ed's handwriting's shaky
as his mortgage payments.
May's quilting, the only thing
her fingers know to do.
Despite the heat, her handiwork
rolls up to her wrinkled chin, almost smothers her.
And here comes Vernon,
just who Ed don't want to hear.
So Dewey's got a new computer.
Tell that to the chamber of commerce.
Another car rolls by. And another.
Someone even waves.
Straw hat's raised in answer, in anger,
then flopped down sideways on Ed's head.
Go help your grandmother, Ed says.
Steam rises from the swamps,
raccoon pans the trash for food,

wood-stork chatters from a cypress branch.
Vernon creeps reluctantly indoors.
May stops her quilting for a kiss,
struggles to remember who exactly is this boy.
Along comes Temple to complain
about the weather and business and his wife.
Ed listens but his ear is cocked for cars the more.
He straightens his straw hat.
Brim holds by a thread.
How long you had that thing? asks Temple.
Forty years, says Ed. It brings me luck.

Oxford

I'm not a scholar,
I'm just passing through.

I haven't a thesis
on Roger Bacon to write.
I'm merely taking in
the splendid architecture
from the Radcliffe Camera
to St Mary's church.

I'm no don, no student,
merely a tourist
with a day to spare,
watching punters in the river,
poking around in
the Bodleian library.

This is part of my education
no doubt
but no fancy degree
comes at the end of it.
Maybe an ale in a pub,
a round of darts,
and a train back to London.

Tomorrow, I'm off
to the Tower of London.
Not to be imprisoned,
tortured or executed.
But surely
you've guessed that already

A New Life In The City

The woman feels what willow trees implore,
The last stroll round the lake, before she leaves
The childhood home, with heavy heart she grieves
For moments turned to ripples at the shore,
That lap on banks until they lap no more.
The days to come are blessed but they are thieves.
Horizon promises but it deceives,
And willows are too downcast to ignore.

The new life cannot meet the old halfway.
It overwhelms it in its reverie,
As most of her says go, a part says stay;
She rests her doubt against the willow tree,
As lowing branches dip to sorrow's sway,
The shadow's weight must do for memory.

Sick Of Love

She's become like one of those government buildings
where I have to go through a metal detector if I want to see her.
Meanwhile, the snow is melting and the buried trash
in all the vacant lots is reemerging.
And the art show at the local gallery is a series of painted urinals.
The weather's perfect – for revolution that is.
So here I go again, braving machine gun fire and mustard gas.
Everything stretches to infinity – the crow flies but I can only
walk.
And she's like a musician's manager, the kind that can't get him
any gigs.
Did I tell you about the time she poured cooking oil into my hair?
Or set fire to my books? Or crowded the bed?
Or said to me, more than once, "Don't bother coming to the
party."
"Or to the open reading." "Or to Brooklyn Heights."
I'm sick of love and the medicine cabinet hasn't been paying
attention.
I'm sick of love. "How can you be?" somebody asks.
That's like being sick of the public library.
That's right. All those books that figure they know the answer to
everything.
I'm sick of tossing condoms into the waste-basket.
She's disillusioned me. I thought the Civil War was over.
But that's her, glaring up at me from one of those faded black
and white photographs.
Whatever side she's on, she insists it's the winning one.
I'm sick of love like I'm sick of meeting new families and hating
every last one of them.

And driving home on snowy roads in winter.
And yes, being the idiot who ends up whitewashing Tom
Sawyer's fence.
Or the second best one in the rom.
Or not knowing what my own drumbeat sounds like.
She insists on picking fruit from the vine for me that's already
rotten.
And when she finally allows me a moment to look up at the stars,
the clouds burst. I'm soaked to the very limit of my endurance.
Likewise, I'm sick of not seeing the butterfly.
Of roaming through the same old Godforsaken haunts.
The hissing green snakes in the trees. The stool and the cap
marked "Idiot."
She's not above leaving me to my nightmares.
Or performing what she calls "occupational therapy" on my
heart.
I'm sick of the politics. I'm even sick of the poetry and that's
hard for me.
And I'm sick of how Picasso's most Cubist of portraits
really do resemble the people I know.
She reads me my rights and then ignores them.
She prefers that I remain shell-shocked at all times.
And then she has the nerve to toss me aside like placenta.
So I'm sick of open-mouthed wonder. Of B flat on the guitar.
Of speaking in tongues. Of arms and torsos, feet and faces.
I'm sick of love. And all else that comes of being alive and
breathing.

Those Illegals

The housekeeper is an illegal alien.
You're sure of it.
When she kneels on the floor,
scouring grit out from the kitchen tiles,
you're watching a criminal in action,
worse than a bank-robber or a swindler,
maybe even than a murderer.

But she's thorough, you'll give her that.
From sink to table, she doesn't leave
a speck of dirt anywhere.
Besides, you can't find anyone local
who works this cheaply, this efficiently.

You'd run her in,
make a stand for law and order,
but laundry doesn't do itself.
You send her back to where
she came from
but there's a not so small matter
of the rugs.
Who's to vacuum
all the plushness
if she's in Guatemala?

But one of these days,
you'll ask to see her papers.
Some night when she's done
picking up yours.

Swamp Mary

To Swamp Mary,
the forest, the cypress marshes,
are like a pharmacy
where everything is free.

And no risk of depleting that bounty.
All shelves are being constantly restocked.

Why waste time
in town emporiums, she says,
when the bitter tea of bark,
or the rot of old black willow,
can soothe the most virulent aches
far more effectively than aspirin.

She grinds up
hickory catkins, meadow holly,
string lily,
into the perfect unguent
for rubbing on sores.

And what she does with
cottonmouth skins, frog legs,
and the gimlet eyes of salamanders
borders on witchcraft.

She says that
she's never been sick a day in her life
and insists that,

if a person gives themselves up to nature
then nature will provide.

She lives in an old fishing shack
where land and water shade into one another
and every breath sucks the heavy heat
into her ancient lungs.

Folks reckon
she's as much Swamp
as she is Mary.

At Eighty-Seven

He'd still strap on his old Gibson guitar,
pluck at the strings with wrinkled fingers,
sing in a deep cackle
the words he strained to remember.

God and the devil,
good women and bad,
barrooms and churches,
poverty and penance –

the same old same old
and always in G.

Eyebrows

The old moneyed family's survival
is all in the way they raise their eyebrows.
Forget the fortune generated
by long shuttered mills.
Try asking them a question.
Or offering an opinion.
Those clumps of hair head northward
even as the eyes stay put.

The skill has been handed down to the children.
Even less subtle than their elders,
their faces seem to expand six inches
to accommodate the sudden separation of body parts.

There's no humility in the genes, young or old,
though there's nobody in the current generations
whose sweat, whose risk-taking, actually earned a dime.
But they're still here.
They cling to their name like it's a lifebelt in the ocean.
If they ever did sink below the surface,
their eyebrows would be the last thing showing.

These Things Happen

These things happen.
Late March rain and I'm
driving alongside a swollen river
which is already overflowing its banks,
and lapping against my tires,
with more threatening puddles up ahead,
but I'm not slowing down
because I need to be some place
at a certain time
though my windshield wipers
are flapping like the wings of flightless birds
and visibility is gray and tree-lined
and suddenly I'm skidding,
aquaplaning, steering one way
while the car goes off in
an opposite direction
and I'm panicking because
the river's moving in on me,
wants to get its grips on
my two ton of metal,
when thankfully I twist
and spin and head off
towards the far side of the road,
into pines, press hard down on
the brake, and stop, near-sideways
on a wet but not flooded surface
and with just a scrape on
the passenger side door
like a notch in a gun of near misses.

These things happen.
I could have drowned.
Instead I sat there in my car
until rescue came.
I felt foolish and ashamed.
But I was pleased that these things happen.
Because there's other things, much worse,
that only happen once.

The Drifter

He could not settle in one place.
Every town was too easily summarized
in a single shot of spit.
And people here turned out to be people there.
None had the allure
of the ones he hadn't met yet.

He moved so often
that movement became his version of standing still.
He could hop a freight
just like the hobos used to do it in the depression.
Or hitchhike,
talk to a truck-driver
until the company started sucking up all
the space and air.

He was no scholar.
And never held a job more than a week.
He got by on very little money.
But he could live off the land,
public or private.
And he camped out where he could,
stared up at the stars at night
wishing for a cheap way for him to get there.

No one knows where he is now
or where he's been
just the time he was around
and how many breaths it took

before he wasn't.
He sure turned restlessness
into a higher calling.

Once some cop told him to move right along.
That got a grin out of him.

Radio

They gathered around the radio then.
Dinner over with, the family retreated to the parlor.
Father turned the knob. Transistors slowly
hummed to life. The solitary speaker cleared its
throat. Then came a singer, female, rousing,
sending the boys off to war with loud and patriotic tonsils.

She had no face, no body, but in their heads she did.
Father rode her cleavage with every high note.
Mother saw her brassy, blonde, but a good girl behind
the makeup. The daughter dreamed herself into high
heels and tight red dress but her vocals less a belter,
more seductive. To the son, she was America
singing right at him. By the time the number finished,
he was ready to fight.

It was still a time of bread-lines, soup kitchens.
Europe was a madhouse. Americans held their breath.
But they had cheesy song, they had kitsch,
they had what moved the heart, they had altos,
they had red hot mamas, they had torch singers,
and, if that didn't stir, there was always
"God Bless America."

The radio shaped the conversation.
It was Stars and Stripes,
It recruited.
It was a huckster selling war bonds.
It was a president's crackling fire.

And when talk couldn't convince,
on came a songstress from the heartland,
catchy numbers you could tap a bayonet to.

Boys died with tunes in their head.
Or they came home, notes rattled,
chords shredded, verses blotted out,
but the chorus, though wounded badly,
still on the tongue.
The radio welcomed them back into their old chair.
Their blood no longer needed,
they sang along to the hit parade.
Television was on the horizon.
Until then, victory would have to do.

Chicago In The Fall

This is not vacation, strictly business.
Lake Michigan fades into the setting sun
fifteen floors below my room.
I eat in the hotel restaurant.
My expense account prefers it that way.
The meal is mild and mediocre enough
to both please and displease no one.
I take my receipt back to the room with me.

But I'm in no mood for an early night.
So I go for a walk, coatless,
shirt snapping like fingers
in the cool lake wind,
hair blowing sideways.
The stores are open along the Golden Mile.
Tourists shop. Credit cards reverberate in wallets and purses.

I head for a blues club.
A candy-coated version of the real thing
but heaven for all that.
The bar is lined with conventioneers.
The stage is sweaty with black chords and voices.

When I leave, I stroll for blocks
with a good time ringing in my ears.
The drunks are out by then -
the playful kind, thankfully.

Tomorrow, I'll be stuck in a room
feigning interest in a slide show
of the latest software lines.
Secrets will retreat
and mock-concentration
will determine my facial expression.

For now, I listen to the rush
of waves hitting sand.
I see lights matching it with the stars,
feel the throb of the traffic,
and the heartbeat of shoe on sidewalk.

This is not what the company's paying for.
But many are the ways
to spend their precious dime.

What A Country

Some dance until they drop.
Some blow steam
like a kettle on a hot plate.
A few are in regular contact
with a guy who tells them
all they need to know.

It's America.
Words come out of some mouths
and are stuffed into others.
Most use soap to get the dirt off.
That isn't always enough.

Some use sex as a blowtorch.
Some shove it down
into their underwear
where it belongs.
Not everyone loves their body.
But it's all they can afford.

It's America.
Not America as people
might have hoped.
But the one where you
get to live
when all other means of existence
are exhausted.

Some take to the streets.
Some crouch down in small rooms.
Some are so religious,
their devil-horns
are uprooted by crosses.

In America,
people grow politicians
in their wombs.
Or stick to their beliefs
like fridge magnets.
Or go undercover
in their own lives.

Some sing a hymn
in praise of themselves.
Some are so homeless,
not even life is their home.
A few, very few,
rise to the top,
look down, way down,
upon the last time they kept their word.

It's America.
50 states
but an endless supply
of states of being.
At this very moment,
I happen to be standing in it.
The sky is overcast.
It's starting to rain.
What other country can say that?

Acknowledgements:

A New Life In The City: The MacGuffin
A Subway Muso: Penumbra
And More Books: Perceptions
Arkansas Truck Stop: Studio 1
Art Attack: Centrifugal Eye
At Eighty Seven: Chronogram
Available For Cat Feeding: Your One Phone Call
Bobcat: The Blotter
Chicago In The Fall: Winamop
Crows: Euphemism
Eyebrows: Phenomenal Literature
Gaits: The Blotter
Gas Station: Subterranean Blue Poetry
Get Born Why Don't You: Sheila-Na-Gig
Guest Of Myself: Door Is A Jar
Hard Times: Fiction Week
I Have A History: Redactions
I Saw Ray: Triggerfish
Identity: Anti-Heroin Chic
Jack Of All Trades: Creosote
Jenna Moves South: Too Well Away
Maine: Misery Tourism
Marie: Mad Swirl
Meet The Folk: Charleston Anvil
Michael's Music Lessons: Havik
Mood For You: San Pedro River Review
My Annoying Self: Zombie Logic
Obligations: Wraparound South
Oxford: Leaves Of Ink

Parental Visit: The Blotter

Picasso Dies At Fifteen: West Trade Review

Poem For It: Hollins Critic

Poetry Class: Abbey

Sick Of Love: Panoplyzine

Stone: Zombie Logic

Swamp Mary: Woven Tales

The Car Came For The Rich Kid: Turk's Head Review

The Cicadas: The Blotter

The Homes Of CEOS: Wraparound South

The Kid: Abbey

The Mistress's Lament: Zombie Logic

The Rhino: Penumbra

The Shakespearean Actor: Studio 1

The Snail: Fireflies Light

The Time Of Your Child: Havik

These Things Happen: Defunkt

This Trunk Must Never Be Removed: Matador Magazine

Those Illegals: Linnet's Wings

Waking In A Fishing Village: Tulip Tree Review

Watching The Monarchs: Open House

Watching The Snake Charmer: Sheila-Na-Gig

What A Country: Off Course

Why I Won't Be With You At Christmas: Multiplicity

Yours, Hilda: Floyd County Moonshine

9 788182 538030